TOM BRADY

The Golden Arm of the Gridiron

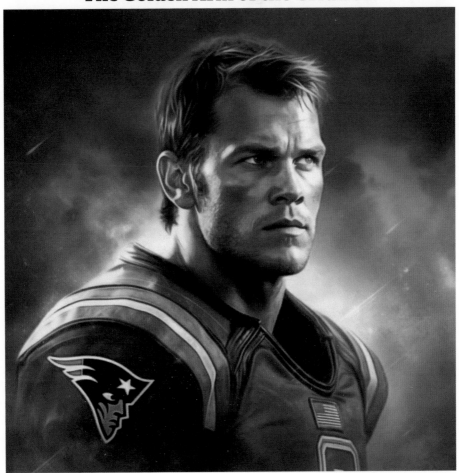

Daniel D. Lee

I. INTRODUCTION

A. INTRODUCTION TO TOM BRADY

Thomas Edward Patrick Brady Jr., better known as Tom Brady, is widely recognized as one of the greatest quarterbacks in the history of the National Football League (NFL). Born on August 3, 1977, in San Mateo, California, Brady's love for football was evident from his early years. Yet, few could have predicted the unprecedented heights this young football enthusiast would eventually reach in the professional realm.

Brady's career is the stuff of legends. It's a journey marked by triumphs and setbacks, with his undeniable talent, relentless work ethic, and remarkable resilience propelling him to the pinnacle of the sport. His name has become synonymous with success in the NFL, with an illustrious career that spans over two decades and includes multiple Super Bowl victories.

Brady's story is not just about a sports superstar's rise to fame and glory; it's also about a determined individual who defied the odds. He wasn't a top pick in the 2000 NFL Draft. Instead, he was the 199th pick, chosen by the New England Patriots in the sixth round. It was from this position of relative obscurity that he launched a career that would reshape the landscape of American football.

In New England, Brady would evolve from a backup quarterback to the face of the franchise, leading the team to six Super Bowl victories. His time with the Patriots marked one of the most successful eras in the history of the franchise and left an indelible impact on the sport. However, even after two decades with the Patriots, Brady wasn't done. He joined the Tampa Bay Buccaneers in 2020, leading them to a Super Bowl victory in his first season with the team, further cementing his legacy.

Off the field, Brady is known for his philanthropy, business ventures, and being a family man. His impact stretches far beyond the gridiron, influencing aspects of popular culture and serving as an inspiration to many.

This book, "Sports Titans: Tom Brady - The Golden Arm of the Gridiron," aims to delve deep into the life and career of Tom Brady, uncovering the man behind the legend, exploring his triumphs and challenges, and revealing how he managed to stay at the top of one of the most physically demanding sports in the world for over two decades. It's a tribute to a sports titan, a man whose golden arm has become a symbol of excellence in the gridiron's fierce battleground.

B. THE SCOPE OF THE BOOK

In "Sports Titans: Tom Brady - The Golden Arm of the Gridiron", our journey extends well beyond the boundary lines of the football field, delving into the life and career of one of the most influential figures in NFL history: Tom Brady.

The book is designed to be a comprehensive guide to understanding the man behind the iconic jersey number 12. It uncovers the nuances of his life, both personal and professional, and puts them into the context of his larger-than-life career.

Starting from his early years, we explore his birth and family background, his early interest in sports, and his athletic achievements in high school and college. This sets the stage for his entry into professional football as the 199th pick in the 2000 NFL Draft, and his initial years with the New England Patriots.

The narrative then focuses on his stellar career, from his first Super Bowl win to building a dynasty with the Patriots, overcoming adversity in the form of injuries, and attaining continued success with multiple championship titles. We follow his journey right up to his decision to leave the Patriots, and his new chapter with the Tampa Bay Buccaneers.

Throughout the book, we pay close attention to Brady's off-field endeavors including his business ventures, philanthropic efforts, and his influence on pop culture. We aim to paint a holistic picture of his life, reflecting not just his sporting prowess, but also his character, values, and the legacy he continues to build.

By the end of "Sports Titans: Tom Brady - The Golden Arm of the Gridiron", readers will have gained a deep and nuanced understanding of Tom Brady, both as an athlete and as a person. This book is more than a sports biography; it's a journey through the life of a man whose golden arm has made an indelible mark on the gridiron, and whose influence extends far beyond it.

C. IMPORTANCE OF BRADY IN SPORTS HISTORY

Tom Brady's significance in sports history cannot be overstated. His contributions have extended far beyond individual records and team championships, reshaping the landscape of the NFL and redefining what it means to be successful in professional sports.

Brady is most commonly recognized for his exceptional ability to perform under pressure, earning him the moniker of the greatest clutch performer in NFL history. His record-breaking performances in numerous Super Bowls have set a benchmark for success in the sport, particularly his ability to orchestrate high-pressure, game-winning drives in the final moments.

However, Brady's importance transcends his on-field achievements. He has redefined the perception of athlete longevity in professional sports. Playing at an elite level well into his 40s, Brady has challenged conventional wisdom about the career span of NFL players, particularly quarterbacks. His meticulous attention to physical conditioning, diet, and mental preparation has influenced younger generations of players who seek to emulate his longevity and success.

Brady's career is also a testament to the power of perseverance. As a sixth-round draft pick, he was far from a guaranteed success in the NFL. His rise from a relative unknown to the most decorated player in the history of the league is a story that resonates with athletes across sports, reinforcing the idea that hard work, dedication, and a never-give-up attitude can overcome initial setbacks or disadvantages.

Furthermore, Brady's influence has also been felt in the realm of team dynamics and leadership. His ability to galvanize his teammates, inspire confidence, and foster a winning culture has been a pivotal aspect of his teams' successes. His leadership style, marked by humility, passion, and an unwavering commitment to the team, serves as a model for athletes in all sports.

Lastly, off the field, Brady's business ventures, philanthropy, and commitment to his family have set an example for professional athletes' roles in society. He has demonstrated how athletes can leverage their fame and success for entrepreneurial endeavors, charitable causes, and promoting positive social values.

In sum, Tom Brady's importance in sports history is multifaceted, extending beyond his unparalleled success on the football field. His career embodies the spirit of competitive sports, characterized by talent, hard work, resilience, leadership, and a commitment to excellence. His influence has left an indelible mark on the NFL and professional sports as a whole, a testament to his status as one of the greatest athletes of his generation.

II. Early Years: The Making of a Star

A. BIRTH AND FAMILY BACKGROUND

Thomas Edward Patrick Brady Jr., known to the world as Tom Brady, was born on August 3, 1977, in San Mateo, California. The only son and the fourth child in a family of five, Tom was born into a close-knit family that placed a high value on athletics and competition.

His father, Tom Brady Sr., was an insurance consultant who passed on his love for sports to his children. Tom Sr. was an avid fan of the San Francisco 49ers, and young Tom Brady grew up cheering for the local team and idolizing its star quarterback, Joe Montana.

His mother, Galynn Patricia, was a remarkable influence on Tom, with her unwavering support and belief in her son's potential playing a significant role in shaping his character and resolve. Galynn, who worked as a flight attendant, battled cancer during the 2016 NFL season, an ordeal that further underscored the family's strength and unity.

Tom's three older sisters, Maureen, Julie, and Nancy, were accomplished athletes in their own right, each excelling in their chosen sports. Growing up in such a competitive environment, Brady developed a deep-seated drive to excel. From a young age, he showcased a competitive spirit and a willingness to put in the work necessary to achieve his goals.

Despite not coming from a family with any professional sports connections, Tom Brady's upbringing was instrumental in molding his sporting character. It was in this nurturing and sports-loving family environment that Brady's love for sports, particularly football, was kindled, setting the stage for his future path as one of the most successful quarterbacks in NFL history.

B. EARLY INTEREST
IN SPORTS

Tom Brady's journey to becoming one of the greatest quarterbacks in NFL history began in the modest surroundings of his hometown, San Mateo, California. His interest in sports sparked at a very young age, showing a natural affinity not just for football, but for baseball and basketball as well.

Growing up in a sports-loving family, the young Brady was often found either with a ball in his hands or watching games on television. His parents, Galynn Patricia and Thomas Brady Sr., were avid sports fans and encouraged their four children to participate in various sports activities. This environment nurtured Tom's interest and, more importantly, his competitive spirit.

Among Brady's earliest memories is attending San Francisco 49ers games with his father. Watching legendary quarterback Joe Montana weave his magic on the field left a profound impact on Brady, inspiring him to pursue football seriously. In fact, he was present at the famous 1981 NFC Championship game, better known as "The Catch" game, where Montana's pass to Dwight Clark secured the 49ers' victory. This event was a turning point in Brady's young life, planting the seeds of a dream that would one day turn him into an NFL superstar.

Brady did not confine his athletic pursuits to football alone. He was also a remarkable baseball player. During his high school years at Junipero Serra High School, he was a left-handed hitting catcher with a strong arm and was even drafted by the Montreal Expos in the 1995 Major League Baseball draft. However, his love for football was stronger, and he decided to commit his future to the gridiron.

Brady's early interest in sports, therefore, was not just a pastime, but a passion that drove him. His early exposure to competitive sports, his innate athletic talent, and his relentless competitive spirit set the stage for his illustrious football career. Even at a young age, it was clear that sports were not just a part of Brady's life, but a calling that would define his future.

C. HIGH SCHOOL YEARS AND ATHLETIC ACHIEVEMENTS

Tom Brady's passion for sports became evident during his high school years at Junipero Serra High School, an all-boys Catholic school in San Mateo, California. This period was instrumental in shaping Brady's athletic career, as he excelled in both football and baseball, demonstrating the potential that would eventually make him a standout in the world of professional sports.

In football, Brady played as a quarterback, showing early signs of the leadership and strategic thinking that would later define his professional career. He was determined and committed, continually honing his skills and understanding of the game. By his senior year, he had made a significant impact on his team, leading them to a respectable 6-4 record and earning All-State and All-Far West honors.

Parallel to his budding football career, Brady also showcased significant talent on the baseball field. As a catcher, he drew attention from Major League Baseball scouts due to his strong arm and batting skills. In fact, Brady was so impressive that he was selected in the 18th round of the 1995 MLB Draft by the Montreal Expos. However, his heart was already set on football, a decision that would prove prophetic in the years to come.

Brady's high school years were not solely focused on athletics. He was known to be a diligent student, balancing his academic responsibilities with his sports commitments. He graduated in 1995 with an impressive resume, both acadically and athletically, setting the stage for his next step: the University of Michigan.

These formative years at Junipero Serra High School were critical in shaping the athlete and man Tom Brady would become. His athletic achievements during this time signaled the early promise of a remarkable sports career, hinting at the legendary status he would eventually attain on the gridiron.

D. COLLEGE YEARS: FOOTBALL AT THE UNIVERSITY OF MICHIGAN

After a successful athletic stint in high school, Tom Brady chose to pursue his love for football at the collegiate level. He enrolled at the University of Michigan in 1995, a choice that would shape the next stage of his football journey and lay the groundwork for his future NFL career.

In his first two years, Brady found himself low on the depth chart, serving as the backup to Brian Griese, who led the Wolverines to a National Championship in 1997. While some might have seen this as a setback, Brady used this time to develop his skills and gain a deeper understanding of the game. His patience and perseverance paid off in his junior year when he was named the starting quarterback for the Wolverines.

Brady's tenure as the starting quarterback wasn't without its trials. In his senior year, he found himself in a heated competition with Drew Henson, a highly touted prospect from Michigan. Despite the pressure, Brady held onto the starting position, demonstrating not just his ability on the field but his leadership and resilience.

His final two seasons at Michigan are remembered for

some remarkable performances, particularly in high-pressure situations. Brady led the Wolverines to victory in the 1999 Orange Bowl and orchestrated multiple come-from-behind victories. His performances showcased his clutch playing ability, a characteristic that would become a hallmark of his professional career.

Off the field, Brady majored in General Studies but was particularly interested in psychology and sociology. These subjects likely influenced his understanding of team dynamics and leadership, elements that would later play significant roles in his professional career.

By the time Brady concluded his career at Michigan, he had set the record for the most pass completions in a season and ranked third in total pass completions in the school's history. However, despite his notable achievements, Brady wasn't considered a top prospect for the upcoming NFL draft. His time at Michigan had been marked by both perseverance and success, a pattern that would repeat itself in the years to come in the NFL.

III. 2000 NFL DRAFT:
THE 199TH PICK

A. PRE-DRAFT EXPECTATIONS

After a successful college career at the University of Michigan, Tom Brady set his sights on the National Football League. However, entering the 2000 NFL Draft, his prospects were far from certain. Despite showing growth and consistency as a quarterback in college, Brady was not considered a top prospect. His physical abilities were not as impressive as some of his peers, and many teams overlooked him due to concerns about his arm strength, mobility, and overall athletic ability.

Despite these doubts, Brady had some strong selling points. He was recognized for his strong leadership, competitiveness, and ability to perform under pressure. His impressive senior year at Michigan, which included leading the Wolverines to an Orange Bowl victory, was a testament to his potential.

Furthermore, Brady had a reputation for being a hard worker with a relentless determination to improve, characteristics that would later define his professional career. His college coach, Lloyd Carr, vouched for his work ethic and football intelligence, noting Brady's commitment to studying game tapes and his understanding of offensive strategies.

However, this praise from his coach and his proven performance under pressure did little to elevate his standing in the eyes of many NFL scouts. As a result, the expectations for Brady leading into the 2000 NFL Draft were modest at best. Many draft analysts projected him as a middle-to-late round pick, reflecting the general uncertainty about his potential in the professional ranks.

Unbeknownst to everyone at the time, this underestimation of Brady would set the stage for one of the greatest draft steals in NFL history. The overlooked prospect would go on to become one of the most accomplished and decorated players the league has ever seen.

B. DRAFT DAY:
BECOMING A PATRIOT

The 2000 NFL Draft was a pivotal moment in Tom Brady's life, marking the beginning of his professional career. However, unlike his future on-field performances, Brady's draft day was far from glamorous. It was a long, anxious day, filled with uncertainty and, eventually, relief and resolve.

Despite a solid career at the University of Michigan, Brady was not among the highly sought-after prospects. The concerns mostly revolved around his lack of mobility and physical strength. His NFL Combine performance didn't help his case either, where he famously ran one of the slowest 40-yard dash times for a quarterback. As a result, Brady watched as six rounds went by, with 198 players selected ahead of him, including six other quarterbacks.

Finally, with the 199th overall pick in the sixth round, the New England Patriots selected Brady. The Patriots, led by head coach Bill Belichick, saw potential in Brady's accuracy, decision-making, and composure under pressure, despite his perceived physical shortcomings.

Brady's reaction to his draft position was one of mixed feelings. On one hand, there was relief that he had been drafted and would have the chance to play in the NFL. On the other hand, there was a deep sense of disappointment and a feeling of being overlooked. This slight would serve as a powerful motivation for Brady, fueling his desire to prove his doubters wrong.

On draft day, Brady famously told Robert Kraft, the owner of the Patriots, that picking him was the best decision the organization had ever made. It was a bold statement from a sixth-round draft pick, but as history would show, it wasn't an exaggeration.

Brady's draft day marked the start of a legendary career, one that would defy expectations and redefine success in the NFL. Despite the initial setback, Brady's determination, work ethic, and self-belief set the stage for his transformation from the 199th pick to one of the greatest players in the history of the sport.

C. INITIAL YEARS WITH THE PATRIOTS

Tom Brady was selected as the 199th pick in the 6th round of the 2000 NFL Draft by the New England Patriots, a moment that would prove to be a turning point not only for Brady, but also for the franchise. As a low draft pick, Brady was not immediately thrust into the limelight; rather, he began his career as the fourth-string quarterback, behind Drew Bledsoe, John Friesz, and Michael Bishop.

Brady's first season with the Patriots was quiet. He saw action in only one game, attempting and completing his first career pass in a lopsided loss to the Detroit Lions. Despite the limited playing time, Brady used his rookie season to learn and grow. He spent countless hours studying playbooks, analyzing game films, and improving his physical conditioning.

In his second year, Brady moved up to the backup quarterback position behind established starter Drew Bledsoe. The 2001 season started ordinarily enough, but everything changed during the second game when Bledsoe suffered a serious injury. Suddenly, Brady, the overlooked 6th round draft pick, was thrust into the starting quarterback position.

Although Brady was relatively unknown and untested, he seized the opportunity. He led the Patriots to an 11-3 record in the remaining games of the season, demonstrating poise, accuracy, and an uncanny ability to perform under pressure. These early successes were a sign of things to come, as Brady's initial years with the Patriots set the stage for an unprecedented era of dominance in the NFL. Little did anyone know at the time, but the quarterback who was once 199th pick in the draft was on the brink of rewriting the record books.

IV. The First Super Bowl: A Star is Born

A. TAKING OVER THE STARTING ROLE

The New England Patriots' decision to draft Tom Brady in 2000 started a new chapter in both his life and the franchise's history. However, his journey from draft day to becoming the team's starting quarterback was not immediate, and it required patience, hard work, and a twist of fate.

Initially, Brady served as the fourth-string quarterback, behind Drew Bledsoe, John Friesz, and Michael Bishop. His rookie year was largely uneventful, with Brady appearing in only one game and throwing just three passes. Yet, Brady didn't let his limited playing time dampen his determination. Instead, he spent the year studying the playbook, improving his physical conditioning, and learning from Bledsoe, the team's veteran starter.

Brady's opportunity came during the second game of the 2001 season in a moment of crisis for the Patriots. Drew Bledsoe, the team's franchise quarterback, suffered a serious injury after a hit from New York Jets linebacker Mo Lewis. With Bledsoe sidelined, the 24-year-old Brady was thrust into the starting role.

Despite the pressure and the challenging circumstances, Brady demonstrated poise and maturity beyond his years. He led the Patriots to an 11-3 record in the remaining 14 games of the regular season. His performances were marked by his precision passing, his ability to read defenses, and, most importantly, his calm and composed demeanor in high-pressure situations.

Brady's takeover of the starting role marked a turning point for the New England Patriots. The young quarterback, once a sixth-round draft pick and fourth on the depth chart, was now leading the team. Little did anyone know that this change would herald the beginning of a dynasty and the rise of one of the greatest quarterbacks in NFL history. Brady's ascension to the starting role is a testament to his readiness to seize the opportunity, his relentless work ethic, and his ability to inspire and lead his team.

B. LEADING THE PATRIOTS TO VICTORY: 2001 SEASON

When Drew Bledsoe suffered a serious injury in the second game of the 2001 season, Tom Brady was thrust into the spotlight as the New England Patriots' starting quarterback. Although his initial performance was modest, Brady quickly grew into his new role, leading the Patriots to an 11-3 record in the remaining games of the regular season.

The 2001 season was marked by Brady's poise and consistency. Despite being a relative newcomer, he demonstrated remarkable maturity and leadership, winning the respect and trust of his teammates. His ability to read defenses, make quick decisions, and deliver accurate passes helped the Patriots transition smoothly despite the sudden change in quarterback.

Brady's real test came in the postseason. His first playoff game was a memorable one, the famous "Tuck Rule" game against the Oakland Raiders. In a blizzard, Brady led the Patriots to a dramatic overtime victory. The game is remembered for a controversial call where what initially appeared to be a Brady fumble was ruled an incomplete pass, giving the Patriots a chance to tie the game and eventually win in overtime.

In the AFC Championship game against the Pittsburgh Steelers, Brady suffered an ankle injury and had to leave the game. However, the Patriots still managed to secure a victory, earning a spot in Super Bowl XXXVI against the heavily favored St. Louis Rams, led by the potent "Greatest Show on Turf" offense.

Despite being underdogs, the Patriots, with Brady back at the helm, managed to stay competitive against the Rams. With the game tied late in the fourth quarter, Brady showcased his exceptional ability to perform under pressure. He led a drive in the final minutes to set up a 48-yard field goal by Adam Vinatieri as time expired, clinching the Patriots' first Super Bowl victory and marking the arrival of a new star in the NFL. Brady, just a year removed from being a backup, was named Super Bowl MVP, a testament to his remarkable rise.

C. SUPER BOWL XXXVI: FIRST CHAMPIONSHIP RING

The conclusion of the 2001 NFL season saw Tom Brady lead the New England Patriots to Super Bowl XXXVI, in what would be the first of many appearances on football's grandest stage. Held in New Orleans on February 3, 2002, the Patriots faced off against the St. Louis Rams, a team that was favored to win and dubbed "The Greatest Show on Turf" for their explosive offense.

Despite the Rams' high-powered offense, the Patriots' defense managed to hold them to only three points in the first half, while Brady helped orchestrate a couple of scoring drives to give New England a surprising 14-3 halftime lead. The Rams, however, fought back in the second half, tying the game at 17-17 with less than two minutes remaining in the fourth quarter.

With 1:21 left on the clock and no timeouts, Brady showcased the poise and leadership that would become his signature. He led the Patriots on a 53-yard drive to set up kicker Adam Vinatieri for a 48-yard field goal attempt. With only seconds remaining, Vinatieri's kick sailed through the uprights, giving the Patriots a 20-17 victory and their first Super Bowl win in franchise history.

Brady's performance in Super Bowl XXXVI was a testament to his composure under pressure. Despite being a young quarterback with only one season of starting experience, Brady demonstrated incredible calm and precision in the game's final drive. His ability to lead his team in the face of a seemingly insurmountable challenge was a glimpse of the greatness that was to come.

For his leadership and efficient performance, Brady was named Super Bowl MVP, becoming the youngest quarterback to ever win a Super Bowl at the age of 24. He completed 16 of 27 passes for 145 yards and a touchdown, but it was his ability to guide his team when it mattered the most that truly stood out.

Super Bowl XXXVI was the first major highlight in Brady's illustrious career. The first championship ring not only marked the beginning of the Patriots dynasty but also the rise of a young quarterback who would go on to become one of the greatest players in NFL history.

D. REFLECTION ON THE IMPACT OF FIRST WIN

The impact of the Patriots' first Super Bowl win, with Tom Brady at the helm, was profound and far-reaching. It marked the beginning of a new era in the NFL, and the dawn of one of the most successful dynasties in professional sports.

For Tom Brady, the win was a vindication of his ability and potential. Despite being overlooked in the draft and starting his career as a backup, Brady proved that he could not only compete at the highest level but could also lead his team to the pinnacle of success. This first Super Bowl win cemented Brady's status as a top-tier quarterback and demonstrated his exceptional ability to perform under pressure. It boosted his confidence and laid the foundation for his future successes.

For the New England Patriots, the victory marked the beginning of an era of dominance. It was their first Super Bowl win in franchise history, a significant achievement that brought newfound respect and attention to the team. The Patriots' triumph also highlighted the astute leadership of head coach Bill Belichick and his successful partnership with Brady.

On a broader level, the 2001 season and Super Bowl victory altered the landscape of the NFL. It showcased the importance of team synergy, effective coaching, and the ability to perform in high-pressure situations, qualities that defined the Patriots under Brady and Belichick. It also highlighted the potential for overlooked or underestimated players to rise to the occasion and make significant impacts.

In the grand scheme of NFL history, the Patriots' first Super Bowl win was a seminal moment. It marked the rise of a new powerhouse and the beginning of Tom Brady's journey to becoming one of the greatest quarterbacks in the history of the sport.

V. BUILDING A DYNASTY: THE PATRIOTS' REIGN

A. OVERVIEW OF 2002-2004 SEASONS: UPS AND DOWNS

The seasons following Tom Brady's first Super Bowl victory were a rollercoaster of highs and lows, providing both personal growth and team development.

The 2002 season was a challenging one for the Patriots. After their Super Bowl XXXVI triumph, the team was met with high expectations. However, they fell short, finishing the season with a 9-7 record and failing to make the playoffs. Brady, however, continued to show improvement. He passed for 3,764 yards, throwing 28 touchdowns and cementing his position as the team's starting quarterback.

The 2003 season began on a sour note with a 31-0 loss to the Buffalo Bills. But the Patriots, led by Brady, quickly turned things around, finishing the regular season with a 14-2 record. Brady continued to grow as a leader, throwing for 3,620 yards and 23 touchdowns during the regular season. The Patriots' renewed success culminated in another Super Bowl appearance in Super Bowl XXXVIII against the Carolina Panthers. Brady's exceptional performance, including throwing for 354 yards and three touchdowns, led the team to a thrilling 32-29 victory and earned him his second Super Bowl MVP award.

The 2004 season saw the Patriots maintain their momentum. They finished the regular season with another strong 14-2 record.

Brady's leadership and consistency were crucial to the Patriots' success. He passed for 3,692 yards and 28 touchdowns during the regular season, demonstrating his continuing growth as a quarterback. The season ended in grand fashion with a victory in Super Bowl XXXIX against the Philadelphia Eagles, securing the Patriots their third Super Bowl championship in four years.

The period from 2002 to 2004 was marked by significant ups and downs for both Brady and the Patriots. It was a time of learning, growth, and ultimate success. Despite facing challenges, Brady continued to evolve as a quarterback and leader, demonstrating his ability to guide his team to victory under various circumstances. The back-to-back Super Bowl victories in the 2003 and 2004 seasons affirmed the Patriots' status as an NFL dynasty, with Brady at the helm.

B. SUPER BOWL XXXVIII: SECOND CHAMPIONSHIP RING

After a 9-7 record and missing the playoffs in the 2002 season, the New England Patriots, led by Tom Brady, were back in championship form for the 2003 season. The team secured a 14-2 record, and Brady was selected for his second Pro Bowl.

The Patriots' journey to Super Bowl XXXVIII was marked by a string of impressive victories, including a thrilling 24-14 win over the Indianapolis Colts in the AFC Championship game, where Brady threw for 237 yards and a touchdown.

Super Bowl XXXVIII, held on February 1, 2004, in Houston, Texas, saw the Patriots face off against the Carolina Panthers. The game would go down as one of the most exciting Super Bowl games in history, featuring a tense back-and-forth contest that remained undecided until the final seconds.

Brady was exceptional throughout the game, showcasing his precision passing, composure, and ability to deliver in the clutch. He completed 32 of 48 passes for 354 yards, throwing three touchdowns, and also leading his team on a crucial drive late in the fourth quarter. With the score tied at 29-29 and just over a minute remaining on the clock, Brady masterfully maneuvered the Patriots down the field to set up a 41-yard field goal by kicker Adam Vinatieri.

Just as he had done two years earlier, Vinatieri converted the game-winning field goal with just seconds remaining, securing a thrilling 32-29 victory for the Patriots. This win marked the second Super Bowl championship for the Patriots and Brady, who was once again named Super Bowl MVP for his outstanding performance.

The victory in Super Bowl XXXVIII further solidified Brady's reputation as a clutch performer and one of the best quarterbacks in the league. His leadership and poise under pressure were key factors in the Patriots' victory, underscoring his pivotal role in the team's success.

C. SUPER BOWL XXXIX: THIRD CHAMPIONSHIP RING

Tom Brady led the New England Patriots to their third Super Bowl victory in four years in Super Bowl XXXIX, firmly establishing the team's status as an NFL dynasty. The game was held on February 6, 2005, at Alltel Stadium in Jacksonville, Florida. The Patriots faced the Philadelphia Eagles, who were led by quarterback Donovan McNabb.

The game was closely contested, with both teams displaying strong defensive performances. Brady, however, managed to break through the Eagles' defense, passing for 236 yards and two touchdowns with no interceptions. His accuracy and decision-making were on full display as he completed 23 of 33 pass attempts.

The Patriots took a 14-7 lead into halftime, thanks to two second-quarter touchdowns, both on Brady passes. The Eagles fought back in the second half, but the Patriots maintained their composure, matching every Eagles score with one of their own.

One key moment came in the fourth quarter when the Patriots were leading 21-14. A crucial drive, orchestrated by Brady, led to a 22-yard field goal by Adam Vinatieri, extending the Patriots' lead to 24-14. Though the Eagles managed to score another touchdown, it was too late to change the game's outcome. The Patriots won 24-21, securing their third Super Bowl title.

Brady's performance in Super Bowl XXXIX was another testament to his leadership and ability to perform under pressure. Even in a game dominated by defense, he found ways to effectively guide his team's offense and consistently put points on the board.

While wide receiver Deion Branch was named the Super Bowl MVP for his 11 receptions and 133 receiving yards, Brady's role in leading the Patriots to victory was unquestionable. The win solidified Brady and the Patriots' status as a true NFL dynasty, with their third championship in four seasons, an accomplishment few teams have achieved in the history of the league. Super Bowl XXXIX marked a significant milestone in Brady's career, highlighting his ability to consistently lead his team to victory on the biggest stage in American football.

D. BRADY'S ROLE IN THE PATRIOTS' DYNASTY

Tom Brady's role in the New England Patriots' dynasty cannot be overstated. From the moment he took over as the team's starting quarterback in 2001, Brady proved to be the catalyst for an era of unprecedented success in Patriots' history.

Over nearly two decades with the Patriots, Brady led the team to six Super Bowl victories and nine AFC Championships, turning the Patriots into the most successful franchise of the 2000s and 2010s. His unflappable poise in high-pressure situations, his laser-like precision as a passer, and his masterful understanding of the game made him an invaluable asset on the field.

More than his physical skills, Brady's leadership and competitive spirit were the driving forces behind the Patriots' dynasty. His relentless work ethic and constant pursuit of perfection set the tone for the entire organization. He was known for his meticulous preparation, studying countless hours of film and holding exhaustive practice sessions with his receivers to build an unparalleled level of chemistry.

Brady's influence extended beyond the gridiron. He was a role model in the locker room, setting a high standard for professionalism and dedication. His ability to galvanize his teammates and inspire them to elevate their own performances was a key factor in the team's sustained success.

Brady's partnership with head coach Bill Belichick was another critical component of the Patriots' dynasty. Together, they formed one of the most successful player-coach duos in NFL history. Their shared commitment to excellence, combined with their strategic acumen, made the Patriots a formidable opponent for any team.

In conclusion, Tom Brady was not just a part of the Patriots' dynasty—he was its driving force. His exceptional skills, leadership, and unwavering dedication played an integral role in the team's remarkable run of success, earning him a place among the greatest quarterbacks in the history of the NFL.

VI. Overcoming Adversity: The 2008 Injury and Comeback

A. THE 2008 INJURY: A CAREER-THREATENING SETBACK

Tom Brady's career took a dramatic turn at the start of the 2008 NFL season. In the opening game against the Kansas City Chiefs on September 7, 2008, Brady suffered a severe knee injury that would abruptly end his season and cast doubt over his future in football.

The injury occurred midway through the first quarter when Chiefs' safety Bernard Pollard hit Brady's left knee. The hit resulted in a torn anterior cruciate ligament (ACL) and a torn medial collateral ligament (MCL) - a combination of injuries known to be particularly debilitating for athletes.

The news of Brady's injury sent shockwaves throughout the sports world. The Patriots, who had just come off an almost perfect 2007 season, losing only in the Super Bowl to the New York Giants, were suddenly without their star quarterback. There were concerns not only about the Patriots' prospects for the season but also about whether Brady, who was 31 at the time, could recover fully and return to his pre-injury performance level.

Brady, known for his competitiveness and determination, met the challenge head-on. He underwent surgery and embarked on an intense rehabilitation process. Despite the severity of the injury, Brady remained focused and committed, approaching his recovery with the same determination that had characterized his football career.

The 2008 season without Brady was difficult for the Patriots, who, despite a respectable 11-5 record with Matt Cassel under center, failed to make the playoffs due to tiebreaker rules. This highlighted Brady's importance to the team and left fans eagerly awaiting his return.

The 2008 injury was indeed a significant setback for Brady. It was the first time he had faced a major health challenge that kept him off the field for an extended period. Yet, the adversity also provided an opportunity for Brady to demonstrate his resilience and determination off the field, traits that would serve him well in his comeback and throughout the rest of his illustrious career.

B. THE RECOVERY PROCESS

The injury that Tom Brady sustained in the opening game of the 2008 season, a torn anterior cruciate ligament (ACL) in his left knee, was a major setback. Such an injury can be career-threatening for a professional athlete, especially one in a high-impact sport like football.

Brady's recovery process was extensive and challenging. Immediately after the injury, he underwent surgery to repair his torn ACL and MCL. The surgery was followed by a grueling rehabilitation program designed to regain strength, mobility, and stability in his knee.

The rehabilitation process involved a combination of physical therapy, strength and conditioning exercises, and gradual reintroduction to football activities. Initially, Brady's therapy focused on reducing swelling and pain, restoring range of motion, and improving muscle control. As his recovery progressed, the focus shifted towards strengthening the muscles around the knee and improving his balance and stability.

Throughout his recovery, Brady demonstrated the same determination and work ethic that had characterized his football career. He adhered to his rehabilitation program diligently, working closely with his physical therapists and trainers to ensure his knee was healing properly.

Beyond the physical recovery, Brady also faced the mental and emotional challenge of dealing with a major injury. He had to confront the uncertainty of whether he would be able to return to his pre-injury level of performance. However, Brady approached this challenge with a positive mindset, viewing the recovery process as an opportunity to come back stronger.

After almost a full year of intense recovery and rehabilitation, Brady was ready to return to the field for the start of the 2009 season. His successful recovery from such a significant injury was a testament to his resilience, determination, and unwavering dedication to his sport. It also set the stage for the next chapter of his illustrious career.

C. THE COMEBACK: 2009 SEASON AND BEYOND

Following his career-threatening injury in 2008, Tom Brady faced the formidable task of recovering his health and returning to the field at an elite level. The 2009 season marked his comeback, and while it was filled with challenges, it also showcased Brady's grit, determination, and ability to bounce back from adversity.

Brady's first game back was the season opener against the Buffalo Bills on September 14, 2009. He showed no signs of hesitation or fear, throwing for 378 yards and leading the Patriots to a 25-24 victory. Despite some early struggles, Brady finished the season with 4,398 passing yards and 28 touchdowns, leading the Patriots to a 10-6 record and a return to the playoffs.

However, the Patriots' 2009 season ended on a disappointing note with a loss to the Baltimore Ravens in the wildcard round. While it was not the triumphant return many had hoped for, it was an important milestone in Brady's recovery and a testament to his resilience.

Brady's comeback wasn't limited to the 2009 season. It carried over into the following years as he continued to perform at an elite level, cementing his legacy as one of the greatest quarterbacks of all time. In 2010, he led the Patriots to a 14-2 record and was awarded the NFL's Most Valuable Player award for the second time in his career, becoming the first player to be selected as MVP by unanimous vote.

The 2008 injury and subsequent comeback were pivotal moments in Brady's career. They tested his resolve, showcased his resilience, and added another layer to his legacy. Despite the initial setback, Brady emerged stronger, further establishing his status as one of the most formidable competitors in the history of the NFL. His performances in the 2009 season and beyond served as a powerful reminder of his dedication, work ethic, and unyielding commitment to the game of football.

D. WINNING THE NFL COMEBACK PLAYER OF THE YEAR

After a grueling recovery from a torn ACL and MCL, Tom Brady made his triumphant return to the field for the 2009 season. His comeback was not just about returning to play—it was about returning to a high level of performance and leading his team once again.

Brady's 2009 season proved to be a resounding success. Despite the doubts and uncertainties that surrounded his comeback, Brady demonstrated that he was still among the elite quarterbacks in the league. He led the Patriots to a 10-6 record and another AFC East title, throwing for 4,398 yards and 28 touchdowns over the course of the season.

Brady's performance was not just impressive in the context of his recent injury; it was impressive by any standard. He ranked among the league leaders in several key passing categories, and his leadership and competitiveness were as strong as ever.

In recognition of his successful comeback, Brady was awarded the NFL Comeback Player of the Year for the 2009 season. The award, given annually by the Associated Press (AP) to a player who has shown outstanding improvement in performance following a period of adversity, was a fitting recognition of Brady's remarkable resilience and determination.

Winning the NFL Comeback Player of the Year was a testament to Brady's grit and perseverance. It affirmed that he was not only back but also still capable of performing at an elite level. It set the stage for the next decade of his career, during which he would continue to build on his legacy as one of the greatest quarterbacks in the history of the NFL.

VII. Continued Success: The Second Wave of Titles

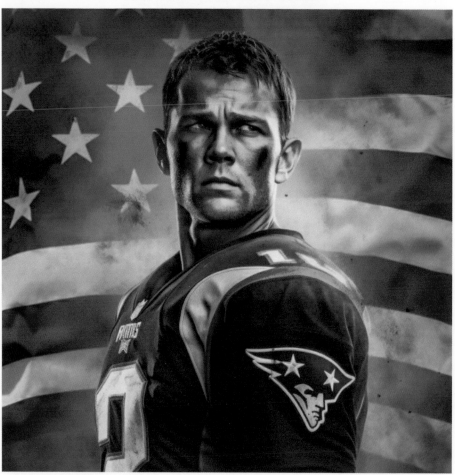

A. LEADING UP TO SUPER BOWL XLIX

The road to Super Bowl XLIX was an eventful journey for Tom Brady and the New England Patriots. The 2014 season saw the Patriots face numerous challenges, but they remained resilient, showcasing their ability to adapt and overcome adversity.

The season started on a shaky note for the Patriots. They had a 2-2 record through the first four weeks, which included a 41-14 blowout loss to the Kansas City Chiefs. Brady himself faced criticism for his performance in these early games, and there were even calls for backup quarterback Jimmy Garoppolo to take over. However, Brady and the Patriots responded in the best way possible - through their play on the field.

Beginning with a convincing 43-17 victory over the Cincinnati Bengals in week 5, the Patriots went on a remarkable run, winning ten of their remaining twelve regular-season games. Brady was instrumental in this resurgence, showcasing his leadership, poise, and exceptional ability to perform under pressure. He finished the regular season with 4,109 passing yards, 33 touchdowns, and just nine interceptions.

In the playoffs, the Patriots defeated the Baltimore Ravens in a thrilling Divisional Round game that saw them overcome two 14-point deficits. Brady threw for 367 yards and three touchdowns in the win. This was followed by a convincing 45-7 victory over the Indianapolis Colts in the AFC Championship Game, a game that would later spark the infamous "Deflategate" controversy.

Despite the brewing controversy, the Patriots remained focused as they prepared for Super Bowl XLIX, set to take place at the University of Phoenix Stadium in Glendale, Arizona. Their opponents were the reigning champions, the Seattle Seahawks, known for their formidable defense, the "Legion of Boom."

The stage was set for one of the most memorable Super Bowls in history, and once again, Tom Brady would find himself at the center of it. His journey to Super Bowl XLIX, filled with ups and downs, served as another testament to his unwavering determination and ability to rise to the occasion.

B. SUPER BOWL XLIX: FOURTH CHAMPIONSHIP RING

Super Bowl XLIX, held on February 1, 2015, would prove to be a historic event for Tom Brady and the New England Patriots. Pitted against the defending champions, the Seattle Seahawks, the Patriots faced a formidable opponent known for its "Legion of Boom" defense.

The 2014 season had been a strong one for the Patriots, as they posted a 12-4 record with Brady throwing for 4,109 yards and 33 touchdowns. Brady's leadership and the team's collective resilience had brought them back to the Super Bowl stage.

The Super Bowl game was a closely contested affair, with both teams showcasing their offensive and defensive prowess. Brady was in top form, demonstrating his exceptional skill and unshakeable composure. Despite throwing two interceptions, he amassed 328 passing yards and four touchdowns.

The game reached a nail-biting climax in the final quarter. With just over two minutes left and the Patriots trailing 24-28, Brady led a decisive 64-yard drive, culminating in a touchdown pass to Julian Edelman. The Patriots led 28-24, but the game was far from over.

The Seahawks, led by quarterback Russell Wilson, were on the verge of scoring in the final seconds of the game. However, in one of the most memorable moments in Super Bowl history, Patriots cornerback Malcolm Butler made a game-saving interception at the goal line. The Patriots won their fourth Super Bowl title, and Brady earned his third Super Bowl MVP award.

Super Bowl XLIX further solidified Brady's legacy as one of the greatest quarterbacks of all time. His performance under pressure, his ability to guide his team to victory against a formidable opponent, and his unyielding determination were all on display, contributing to the Patriots' success and earning him his fourth championship ring.

C. THE ROAD TO SUPER BOWL LI

The 2016 season was a tumultuous one for Tom Brady and the New England Patriots, marked by both controversy and remarkable success. The path to Super Bowl LI was anything but smooth, yet it ultimately led to one of the most dramatic and memorable games in NFL history.

The season began with Brady serving a four-game suspension as a result of the infamous "Deflategate" scandal stemming from the AFC Championship Game during the previous season. Despite the controversy and the enforced absence of their star quarterback, the Patriots managed to start the season strong with a 3-1 record.

Brady returned in Week 5 with a vengeance, leading the Patriots to an impressive 33-13 victory over the Cleveland Browns. It marked the start of an incredible comeback season for Brady, who, at age 39, played some of the best football of his career. In just 12 games, he threw for 3,554 yards and 28 touchdowns, with a mere 2 interceptions, resulting in the best touchdown-to-interception ratio in NFL history.

With Brady at the helm, the Patriots continued their dominance, ending the regular season with a league-best 14-2 record. The Patriots' success carried into the playoffs where they secured decisive victories against the Houston Texans and the Pittsburgh Steelers in the Divisional Round and AFC Championship Game, respectively.

The Patriots' journey to Super Bowl LI was a testament to

their resilience and ability to overcome adversity. From the initial setback of Brady's suspension to the challenges they faced throughout the season, the team proved their mettle time and again, always finding ways to win.

Their opponent for Super Bowl LI would be the Atlanta Falcons, led by MVP quarterback Matt Ryan. With the stage set for a thrilling matchup, the Patriots were poised for a chance at their fifth Super Bowl title and another historic performance from Tom Brady. Little did anyone know that this Super Bowl would turn out to be one of the most dramatic and unforgettable games in NFL history.

D. SUPER BOWL LI: FIFTH CHAMPIONSHIP RING AND HISTORIC COMEBACK

Super Bowl LI, played on February 5, 2017, at NRG Stadium in Houston, Texas, will forever be remembered as one of the greatest games in NFL history, primarily due to a historic comeback led by Tom Brady and the New England Patriots.

The game started in favor of the Atlanta Falcons, who quickly built a commanding 28-3 lead in the third quarter. The Falcons' offense, led by MVP quarterback Matt Ryan, seemed unstoppable, and the Patriots found themselves on the brink of a crushing defeat.

However, with less than two minutes remaining in the third quarter, the Patriots began to mount what seemed an impossible comeback. Brady, refusing to accept defeat, spearheaded a series of scoring drives. He connected with James White for a touchdown, followed by a successful two-point conversion, cutting the deficit to 16 points.

The fourth quarter saw the Patriots' momentum continue to build. Brady led another touchdown drive, this time ending with a six-yard touchdown pass to Danny Amendola, followed by another successful two-point conversion. Suddenly, the Patriots were within one score of tying the game.

With just under four minutes remaining in regulation, Brady orchestrated a 91-yard drive, culminating in a one-yard touchdown run by James White. Another successful two-point conversion tied the game at 28-28, completing the largest comeback in Super Bowl history and sending the game into overtime for the first time ever.

In overtime, the Patriots won the coin toss and elected to receive. Brady, displaying his typical poise and determination, led the Patriots down the field. The drive ended with a two-yard touchdown run by James White, sealing the 34-28 victory and earning the Patriots their fifth Super Bowl title.

Brady finished the game with a Super Bowl record 466 passing yards, along with two touchdowns and one interception, earning his fourth Super Bowl MVP award. His performance in Super Bowl LI was a testament to his unyielding perseverance and competitiveness. Despite facing a seemingly insurmountable deficit, Brady never wavered, leading his team to an unprecedented comeback victory and further solidifying his legacy as one of the greatest quarterbacks in NFL history.

VIII. The End of an Era: Leaving the Patriots

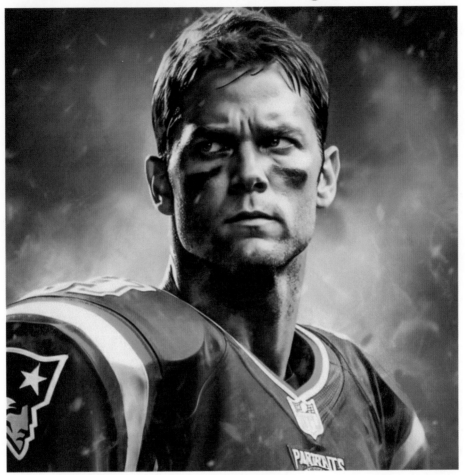

A. THE 2019 SEASON: CHALLENGES AND STRUGGLES

The 2019 season was a challenging one for Tom Brady and the New England Patriots. Despite starting strong with an 8-0 record, the team began to struggle in the second half of the season. Several key players battled injuries, and the offense seemed to lack the consistency and dynamism of previous years.

Brady himself faced challenges. At 42 years old, he was one of the oldest starting quarterbacks in the league, and questions about his age and durability began to emerge. While his leadership and competitiveness remained unimpeachable, his statistical performance saw a slight decline. Brady finished the season with 4,057 passing yards and 24 touchdowns, with his passer rating dropping to 88.0, his lowest since the 2013 season.

The Patriots finished the regular season with a 12-4 record, enough to secure the AFC East title but not enough to earn a first-round bye in the playoffs. Their postseason run was cut short with a loss to the Tennessee Titans in the AFC Wild Card round. This marked the earliest playoff exit for the Patriots in a decade.

Beyond the on-field challenges, there were signs of increasing tension off the field. Rumors of Brady's impending departure from the Patriots began to circulate. The quarterback, who was set to become a free agent in the offseason, remained noncommittal about his future with the team.

The 2019 season was a departure from the sustained success that the Patriots had enjoyed for nearly two decades. Despite the challenges and struggles, Brady's leadership and determination never wavered. He continued to demonstrate his resilience in the face of adversity, setting the stage for the next chapter in his remarkable career.

B. THE DECISION TO LEAVE: END OF A TWO-DECADE ERA

After two decades of unparalleled success with the New England Patriots, Tom Brady made the momentous decision to leave the franchise where he had built his legendary career. The announcement, made on March 17, 2020, marked the end of an era in NFL history and sent shockwaves throughout the world of sports.

Brady's decision to part ways with the Patriots came after a challenging 2019 season. The Patriots started strong but struggled in the latter part of the season. They ended with a 12-4 record, losing to the Tennessee Titans in the wildcard round of the playoffs, their earliest exit since the 2009 season. Brady, who was 42 at the time, had a statistically uneven year, leading to speculation about his future.

In March 2020, Brady announced his decision to leave the Patriots via social media. In his posts, he thanked the Patriots organization, his coaches, his teammates, and the fans for their unwavering support over the past 20 years. He expressed his gratitude for the unforgettable experiences and the lifelong relationships he had developed during his time in New England.

Brady's departure from the Patriots marked the end of one of the most successful partnerships in sports history. Over 20 seasons, Brady, along with head coach Bill Belichick, had transformed the Patriots into a dynasty, winning six Super Bowl titles and establishing a culture of sustained excellence.

However, at the age of 42, and with his contract at New England expiring, Brady was ready for a new challenge. His decision to leave the Patriots signaled a bold new chapter in his career, demonstrating his desire to prove that his success was not solely a product of the Patriots' system. The next stage of Brady's career would take him south, to the Tampa Bay Buccaneers, and yet another remarkable chapter of his storied career was about to be written.

C. REFLECTION ON BRADY-PATRIOTS PARTNERSHIP

The partnership between Tom Brady and the New England Patriots is one of the most successful in the history of professional sports. Spanning two decades, it was marked by unprecedented success, including six Super Bowl victories, nine AFC Championships, and 17 AFC East titles.

The Brady-Patriots era was defined by a shared commitment to excellence, a relentless pursuit of victory, and an unwavering dedication to the team. Brady, together with head coach Bill Belichick, transformed the Patriots from a struggling franchise into a model of consistency and success.

Brady's role in this partnership cannot be overstated. His exceptional skills, competitive drive, and leadership were instrumental in the Patriots' success. He set numerous records, won multiple MVP awards, and cemented his legacy as one of the greatest quarterbacks of all time.

However, the Brady-Patriots partnership was more than just about on-field achievements. Brady embodied the "Patriot Way" – a culture of discipline, preparation, and selflessness. His work ethic, professionalism, and team-first attitude set the tone for the entire organization.

Despite the success, the partnership was not without its

challenges. There were periods of tension and uncertainty, particularly towards the end. The 2019 season, marked by on-field struggles and off-field speculation about Brady's future, signaled that change was on the horizon.

When Brady announced his decision to leave the Patriots in March 2020, it marked the end of an era. While it was a significant change for both Brady and the Patriots, their shared legacy remains intact. The Brady-Patriots partnership will forever be remembered as a golden era in the annals of the NFL, a testament to what can be achieved through talent, dedication, and a shared commitment to excellence.

IX. A New Chapter: The Tampa Bay Buccaneers

A. JOINING THE BUCCANEERS: A NEW TEAM, A NEW CHALLENGE

Tom Brady's decision to sign with the Tampa Bay Buccaneers in March 2020 marked a new and exciting chapter in his illustrious career. After two decades with the New England Patriots, Brady was ready to embark on a new journey, testing his abilities in a new environment with a new team.

The Buccaneers, a franchise with a mixed history of success, had not made the playoffs since the 2007 season. Yet, the team was brimming with potential, boasting a roster of talented players, including wide receivers Mike Evans and Chris Godwin, tight end O.J. Howard, and a promising defense.

Brady's arrival in Tampa Bay was met with great enthusiasm and high expectations. Despite being 43 years old, he was seen as the missing piece in the puzzle, the leader who could harness the team's potential and guide them to success.

Brady's move was more than a simple change of scenery. It presented a unique set of challenges, including acclimating to a new playbook under head coach Bruce Arians and offensive coordinator Byron Leftwich. He also had to build rapport with a new set of teammates, establish his leadership within the locker room, and adapt to a new city and lifestyle.

Moreover, the COVID-19 pandemic added an additional layer of complexity to Brady's transition. The pandemic led to the cancellation of preseason games and limited in-person team activities, which restricted Brady's opportunities to practice with his new teammates.

However, if there's anything Brady had proven over his career, it's that he thrives in the face of adversity. The 2020 season was shaping up to be one of the most intriguing and challenging of his career. As he donned the Buccaneers' red and pewter for the first time, a new era had begun – not only for Brady but also for the Buccaneers and the entire NFL.

B. THE 2020 SEASON: ADJUSTING TO A NEW TEAM

Tom Brady's move to the Tampa Bay Buccaneers for the 2020 season was one of the most significant transitions of his career. After 20 years with the New England Patriots, Brady was faced with the task of adjusting to a new team, a new system, and a new set of teammates.

The 2020 season presented unique challenges due to the COVID-19 pandemic. Traditional offseason activities, such as mini-camps and preseason games, were canceled or modified. This made Brady's transition to the Buccaneers even more challenging, as he had limited time to develop chemistry with his new teammates and learn coach Bruce Arians' offensive system.

Despite these challenges, Brady approached the 2020 season with his characteristic determination and work ethic. He quickly established himself as a leader within the Buccaneers organization, bringing his experience, competitiveness, and high standards to his new team.

On the field, Brady's performance was strong. He threw for 4,633 yards and 40 touchdowns, leading the Buccaneers to an 11-5 record and their first playoff appearance since 2007. There were moments of adjustment, as Brady worked to adapt to Arians' more aggressive, downfield passing attack, but his play improved as the season progressed.

Off the field, Brady worked diligently to build relationships with his new teammates. He organized private workouts during the offseason and developed a strong rapport with receivers like Mike Evans, Chris Godwin, and Rob Gronkowski, who came out of retirement to join Brady in Tampa Bay.

The 2020 season was a testament to Brady's adaptability and leadership. His successful transition to the Buccaneers demonstrated his ability to overcome challenges and excel in a new environment. The stage was set for Brady to once again compete for a Super Bowl title, this time in a different uniform.

C. SUPER BOWL LV: SEVENTH CHAMPIONSHIP RING

Super Bowl LV, played on February 7, 2021, at Raymond James Stadium in Tampa, Florida, marked yet another career-defining moment for Tom Brady. In his first season with the Tampa Bay Buccaneers, Brady led the team to the pinnacle of NFL success, earning his seventh Super Bowl ring in a game that further solidified his legacy as one of the greatest football players of all time.

The Buccaneers faced off against the Kansas City Chiefs, led by dynamic young quarterback Patrick Mahomes. The Chiefs, the defending Super Bowl champions, were favored to win, but Brady and the Buccaneers had other plans.

The game was a showcase of the Buccaneers' dominance, with Brady expertly leading his team's offense while Tampa Bay's defense stifled the Chiefs' usually explosive attack. Brady connected with old Patriots teammate Rob Gronkowski for two touchdowns in the first half, and Antonio Brown added another touchdown before halftime. By the end of the game, Brady had thrown for 201 yards and three touchdowns, leading the Buccaneers to a 31-9 victory.

Brady's performance earned him Super Bowl MVP honors for the fifth time in his career. At age 43, he became the oldest player to ever win the award. However, it wasn't just Brady's on-field performance that stood out. His leadership and ability to galvanize the Buccaneers throughout the season, culminating in their Super Bowl victory, was truly remarkable.

With this win, Brady surpassed his own record for the most Super Bowl wins by a quarterback, and also surpassed the record for the most Super Bowl wins by a single franchise, as his seven rings are more than any one team has achieved.

Super Bowl LV was the crowning achievement of Brady's first season with the Buccaneers, proving that even in a new environment, his winning ways remained unchanged. The victory served as a testament to Brady's enduring greatness, his ability to adapt, and his unyielding drive to win.

D. REFLECTION ON BRADY'S CONTINUED SUCCESS

Tom Brady's continued success, even after leaving the New England Patriots for the Tampa Bay Buccaneers, is a testament to his talent, perseverance, and commitment to excellence. It defies the typical trajectory of professional athletes, particularly in a sport as physically demanding as football.

At an age when most players have long since retired, Brady continues to perform at an elite level. His physical conditioning, meticulous preparation, and unparalleled understanding of the game have allowed him to extend his career and remain competitive.

Brady's success with the Buccaneers reaffirms his status as one of the greatest quarterbacks of all time. He has shown that his achievements are not solely a product of the system or team he was part of in New England. Instead, his performance has demonstrated that his success is largely due to his own abilities, work ethic, and leadership.

Moreover, Brady's continued success underscores his ability to adapt to new circumstances and challenges. Transitioning to a new team and a new system is not easy, especially without a traditional offseason. Yet, Brady has managed to lead the Buccaneers to a successful season, further cementing his legacy.

Brady's career is a study in sustained excellence. His continued success serves as a powerful reminder that age is just a number, that greatness is transferable, and that with talent, hard work, and a relentless pursuit of victory, it's possible to defy the odds and rewrite the narrative.

In the pantheon of NFL greats, Brady's name stands out not just for his record-breaking statistics and multiple championships, but also for his remarkable longevity and sustained success. Regardless of team or circumstance, he has consistently found ways to win and has set a standard of excellence that future generations will strive to match.

X. LEGACY AND IMPACT

A. BRADY'S INFLUENCE ON THE GAME OF FOOTBALL

Tom Brady's influence on the game of football is profound and multi-faceted, reshaping the NFL and leaving an indelible mark on the sport. Over a career spanning more than two decades, he has set numerous records, won multiple championships, and changed perceptions about the longevity of a quarterback's career.

Brady's remarkable consistency and competitiveness have set new standards for quarterbacks. His ability to perform at an elite level well into his 40s has expanded the horizons for how long a quarterback can play in the NFL. His meticulous attention to fitness, nutrition, and preparation have become a blueprint for other players hoping to extend their careers.

His success as a late-round draft pick has also had a significant impact. As the 199th pick in the 2000 NFL Draft, Brady was far from a sure bet. Yet his trajectory from a backup quarterback to one of the greatest players in NFL history has served as an inspiration for many young players. It's a reminder that draft position doesn't define a player's potential and that perseverance, hard work, and a relentless drive to improve can lead to extraordinary achievements.

Furthermore, Brady's impact extends to the tactical aspects of the game. His mastery of the quarterback position, his understanding of the game, and his ability to read defenses and make quick decisions have been instrumental in the evolution of offensive strategies in the NFL. His success in various offensive systems has shown the importance of a versatile and adaptive quarterback.

Brady's influence can also be seen in the next generation of quarterbacks, who look up to him as a role model and benchmark for success. His legacy is reflected in countless young players who aspire to emulate his achievements and his approach to the game.

Finally, Brady's influence is evident in the culture of winning he instilled in the Patriots, and later the Buccaneers. His leadership, competitiveness, and commitment to excellence have had a profound impact on these teams, fostering a winning mentality that has led to sustained success.

In summary, Tom Brady's influence on the game of football is vast and enduring. He has not only set new records and won numerous titles but also inspired future generations, changed perceptions about career longevity, and left a lasting impact on the tactical and cultural aspects of the game.

B. INFLUENCE ON TEAMMATES AND COACHES

Tom Brady's influence extends far beyond his own performance on the field. Throughout his career, he has had a profound impact on his teammates and coaches, shaping the culture of the teams he has been part of and setting a high standard for performance and professionalism.

Brady's work ethic is legendary. His rigorous training regime, meticulous preparation, and unyielding commitment to improvement have set the bar for his teammates. He is often the first player to arrive at the facility and the last to leave, demonstrating a level of dedication that has earned him the respect of his peers.

Brady also has a unique ability to inspire and motivate those around him. His competitive fire and intense desire to win are contagious, fostering a culture of competitiveness and resilience within his teams. He has a knack for building strong relationships with his teammates, fostering a sense of camaraderie and mutual respect.

Coaches, too, have been influenced by Brady. His deep understanding of the game, ability to read defenses, and meticulous preparation make him an invaluable asset. He has often been described as a coach on the field, and his input and insights have undoubtedly shaped the strategies and game plans of the teams he has been part of.

Furthermore, Brady's leadership extends beyond the realm of football. He has been a mentor to many younger players, guiding them in their careers and helping them navigate the challenges of life in the NFL. His philanthropic efforts and commitment to community service have also had a significant impact, setting an example for his teammates to follow.

Overall, Brady's influence on his teammates and coaches is as significant as his on-field achievements. His work ethic, leadership, and commitment to excellence have left an indelible mark on the teams he has been part of and have contributed significantly to his sustained success in the NFL.

C. OFF-FIELD ENDEAVORS: BUSINESS AND PHILANTHROPY

Away from the gridiron, Tom Brady has pursued a variety of business ventures and philanthropic activities, further extending his influence beyond the world of football.

In business, Brady has established himself as a health and wellness entrepreneur. In 2013, he launched TB12, a performance lifestyle brand that promotes a holistic approach to health and wellness, inspired by Brady's own training methods. TB12 offers a variety of products and services, including nutritional supplements, fitness equipment, and personalized training programs. This venture reflects Brady's commitment to healthy living and his desire to help others achieve their performance goals.

Brady has also partnered with various brands throughout his career, endorsing products ranging from watches to cars. His high profile and success on the field have made him a sought-after brand ambassador, and he has leveraged his celebrity status to promote products he believes in.

In the realm of philanthropy, Brady has shown a strong commitment to giving back to the community. He has been involved with numerous charitable organizations, using his platform to raise awareness and funds for causes close to his heart.

One of the most notable examples of Brady's philanthropy is his long-standing relationship with Best Buddies International, a nonprofit organization dedicated to enhancing the lives of people with intellectual and developmental disabilities. Brady has been a vocal advocate for the organization, participating in fundraising events and serving as an honorary co-chair for their annual challenge event.

Brady has also been involved with the Make-A-Wish Foundation, granting wishes for children with critical illnesses, and he has supported various other charities related to children's health and education.

Moreover, Brady has used his platform to respond to societal issues and natural disasters. He has donated significant funds to relief efforts in the wake of hurricanes and has spoken out on social issues.

In summary, Tom Brady's off-field endeavors reveal a man committed to using his platform and resources for the betterment of others. His business ventures reflect his passion for health and wellness, while his philanthropic efforts underscore a deep sense of social responsibility.

D. IMPACT ON POP CULTURE

Tom Brady's influence extends beyond the gridiron and into the realm of popular culture. His success, charisma, and high-profile personal life have made him a prominent figure in American society.

Brady's status as one of the most successful quarterbacks in NFL history has made him a household name. His image has been featured in countless advertisements and endorsements, from luxury watches to athletic wear. His influence in advertising and marketing has made him one of the most recognizable faces in the world of sports.

Brady's high-profile marriage to supermodel Gisele Bündchen has further elevated his status in popular culture. The couple's glamorous lifestyle, combined with their philanthropic endeavors, has been a source of fascination for the public and the media, often landing them in the spotlight.

Brady has also made appearances in various TV shows and films, including "Family Guy," "Entourage," and "Ted 2," further cementing his place in popular culture. His unique diet and fitness regimen, often referred to as the TB12 Method, has also garnered attention, inspiring books and promoting a focus on wellness and longevity in sports and beyond.

Brady's impact on pop culture is reflective of his success on and off the field. His iconic status in the NFL, combined with his visibility in media and advertising, his high-profile personal life, and his influence in the world of health and wellness, has made him a significant figure in popular culture. His influence extends beyond football fans, reaching into various aspects of American society.

XI. Conclusion: The Golden Arm of the Gridiron

A. REFLECTION ON BRADY'S CAREER AND ACHIEVEMENTS

Reflecting on Tom Brady's career and achievements presents an awe-inspiring overview of one of the most successful careers in the history of professional sports. Spanning over two decades, Brady's journey is characterized by relentless dedication, extraordinary competitiveness, and an unwavering commitment to excellence.

Brady's NFL journey began as an underdog story, being drafted as the 199th pick in the 2000 NFL Draft by the New England Patriots. From these humble beginnings, he ascended to the zenith of NFL stardom, winning seven Super Bowl titles and earning numerous individual accolades. His remarkable ability to perform under pressure and his penchant for leading game-winning drives in critical situations cemented his reputation as one of the most clutch performers in sports history.

What sets Brady apart, even more, is his longevity and sustained excellence. Even into his 40s, he remained at the pinnacle of the sport, defying the traditional career arc of NFL quarterbacks. His meticulous preparation, rigorous fitness regimen, and mental toughness have enabled him to maintain an elite level of performance, redefining what is possible for athletes in terms of career length and productivity.

His move from the Patriots to the Buccaneers in 2020 and the subsequent Super Bowl win in his first season with the new team reinforced his greatness. It was a testament to his leadership, adaptability, and the unique ability to cultivate a winning culture.

Off the field, Brady has made significant contributions through his business ventures and philanthropic efforts. His TB12 brand promotes a holistic approach to health and wellness, embodying Brady's own principles around physical fitness and mental preparation. In philanthropy, Brady's work with organizations like Best Buddies International and the Make-A-Wish Foundation reflects his commitment to giving back and making a positive impact on the community.

In conclusion, Tom Brady's career and achievements paint the portrait of a man who has not only reached the pinnacle of his profession but also used his platform to inspire others, promote health and wellness, and contribute to societal good. His legacy extends far beyond his on-field accomplishments, reflecting a career and life characterized by determination, excellence, and a lasting impact on the game of football and beyond.

B. BRADY'S PLACE
IN NFL HISTORY

Tom Brady's place in NFL history is indisputable. With numerous records, accolades, and a career spanning over two decades, he has established himself as one of the greatest quarterbacks of all time, if not the greatest.

Brady's record of seven Super Bowl victories as a starting quarterback is unprecedented in the NFL. His numerous MVP awards, Pro Bowl selections, and numerous other individual accolades further attest to his extraordinary skill and consistency.

Brady holds several significant NFL records, including most career passing touchdowns and most career passing yards. His playoff success is unparalleled, with the most playoff wins, touchdowns, and yards of any player in history.

Beyond his statistical achievements, Brady has had a profound impact on the game of football. His competitiveness, poise under pressure, and ability to perform at a high level late into his career have redefined expectations for quarterbacks and players in general. His approach to training, nutrition, and preparation has influenced players across the league and could have a lasting impact on how athletes take care of their bodies and extend their careers.

Perhaps most importantly, Brady has consistently been a winner. Regardless of the team, the coach, or the system, he has found a way to win games and championships. His ability to lead his teams to victory in critical moments, often in dramatic fashion, is a defining feature of his career.

Brady's career has transcended the sport. He is not just a football player but a cultural icon. His impact on the game, his influence off the field, and his success against the odds make him a seminal figure in NFL history. His story is one of perseverance, excellence, and an unwavering will to win, making him a model for future generations of players.

C. LOOKING FORWARD: TOM BRADY'S LEGACY

As we look forward, Tom Brady's legacy is one that will endure for generations to come. His name will be forever etched in the annals of the National Football League and the broader world of sports as a player whose performance and impact transcended the game of football.

Brady's on-field accomplishments, including his record seven Super Bowl victories and numerous individual accolades, will continue to be benchmarks for future athletes. His competitive spirit, unwavering determination, and ability to perform under pressure have already inspired a new generation of players. The "Brady effect" will likely continue to influence the game, as future quarterbacks and other football players seek to emulate his winning mentality and the standards he set on and off the field.

Beyond his athletic prowess, Brady's approach to physical conditioning and mental preparation will continue to influence how athletes train and prepare for their sports. His TB12 brand, promoting holistic health and wellness, may shape the future of athletic training and nutrition, emphasizing sustainability, flexibility, and mental strength alongside traditional strength and conditioning practices.

In terms of his character and leadership, Brady's legacy will endure as an example of humility, resilience, and unselfishness.

DANIEL D. LEE

Despite his enormous success, he has remained grounded and focused, always putting the team's success ahead of his own. His journey from a sixth-round draft pick to the greatest quarterback of all time is a powerful lesson in perseverance, demonstrating that success is not determined by where one starts but by one's commitment to continual growth and improvement.

Lastly, Brady's philanthropic endeavors and his commitment to using his platform for societal good set an example for other athletes. His work with charitable organizations and his efforts to raise awareness and funds for various causes show that being a successful athlete also involves contributing positively to society.

In conclusion, as we look forward to Tom Brady's legacy, it is clear that his impact will be felt far beyond the football field. His records may one day be broken, but his influence on the sport, his contributions to health and wellness, his inspirational journey, and his commitment to societal good will remain a significant part of his enduring legacy.

XII. Appendices

A. CAREER STATISTICS AND RECORDS

Through the end of the 2020 NFL season, Tom Brady has made numerous remarkable achievements:

Career Passing Yards: As of the end of the 2020 season, Brady had thrown for 79,204 yards, the most in NFL history.

Career Passing Touchdowns: Brady has thrown 581 regular-season touchdown passes, the most in NFL history.

Super Bowl Victories: Brady has won the Super Bowl seven times (Super Bowl XXXVI, XXXVIII, XXXIX, XLIX, LI, LIII, and LV), more than any other player in NFL history.

Super Bowl MVPs: Brady has been named the Super Bowl Most Valuable Player (MVP) four times (Super Bowl XXXVI, XXXVIII, XLIX, and LI), tied with Joe Montana for the most in history.

Regular-Season Victories by a Quarterback: Brady has 230 regular-season wins, the most of any quarterback in NFL history.

Playoff Victories by a Quarterback: Brady has 34 playoff victories, the most of any quarterback in NFL history.

Career 4th Quarter Comebacks/Game-Winning Drives: Brady has led his team to 48 4th quarter comebacks and 60 game-winning drives in his career.

Pro Bowl Selections: Brady has been selected to the Pro Bowl 14 times in his career.

NFL MVP Awards: Brady has been named the NFL's Most Valuable Player three times (2007, 2010, and 2017).

Passing Yards in a Single Season: Brady threw for 5,235 yards in the 2011 season, the fifth-most in a single season in NFL history.

Brady's records are a testament to his longevity, skill, and success as a quarterback. His impact on the NFL has been profound, and his records are likely to stand for many years to come.

B. AWARDS AND ACCOLADES

Throughout his illustrious career, Tom Brady has earned an array of awards and accolades that underscore his exceptional talent, skill, and leadership on the football field. Below are some of the most notable recognitions:

Super Bowl Championships (7): Brady has won seven Super Bowl titles, more than any player in NFL history. His wins came in Super Bowls XXXVI, XXXVIII, XXXIX, XLIX, LI, LIII, and LV.

Super Bowl MVP Awards (5): Brady has been named the Super Bowl Most Valuable Player five times, another record. He received this award for his performances in Super Bowls XXXVI, XXXVIII, XLIX, LI, and LV.

NFL Most Valuable Player (3): Brady has been awarded the NFL's Most Valuable Player award three times, in 2007, 2010, and 2017.

Pro Bowl Selections (14): Brady has been selected to the Pro Bowl, the NFL's annual all-star game, 14 times over the course of his career.

NFL All-Pro First Team (3): Brady has been named to the NFL's All-Pro First Team three times, which recognizes the top players at each position for the season.

NFL Comeback Player of the Year (1): Following a season-ending injury in 2008, Brady returned in 2009 to win the NFL's Comeback Player of the Year award.

Bert Bell Award (2): Brady has won the Bert Bell Award, given to the NFL's player of the year, twice.

Associated Press Male Athlete of the Year (2): Brady was named the AP Male Athlete of the Year in 2007 and 2010.

Sports Illustrated Sportsperson of the Year (2): Brady won the Sports Illustrated Sportsperson of the Year award in 2005 and 2017.

NFL passing yards leader (3): Brady led the NFL in passing yards in 2005, 2007, and 2017.

NFL passing touchdowns leader (4): Brady led the NFL in passing touchdowns in 2002, 2007, 2010, and 2015.

These awards and accolades highlight Brady's extraordinary accomplishments and his standing as one of the greatest players in the history of the NFL. His exceptional talent, skill, leadership, and ability to perform under pressure have been recognized and celebrated throughout his remarkable career.

C. PERSONAL LIFE: FAMILY, INTERESTS, AND VALUES

Tom Brady's personal life is characterized by strong family ties, diverse interests, and a set of values that have guided him throughout his life and career.

Family: Brady is a devoted family man. He is married to Brazilian supermodel Gisele Bündchen, and together they have two children, Benjamin and Vivian. Brady also has a son named John (Jack) from his previous relationship with actress Bridget Moynahan. Despite the demands of his professional career, Brady often speaks about the importance of family and makes it a point to spend quality time with his children and wife. He and Gisele are known for sharing snippets of their family life on social media, often highlighting outdoor adventures and shared moments of celebration.

Interests: Brady has a variety of interests outside of football. He is passionate about health and wellness, which led to the creation of his TB12 brand. He also has an interest in fashion, which has been reflected in his various endorsement deals and public appearances. In addition, Brady is an avid golfer and has participated in several celebrity golf tournaments. He has also expressed a love for surfing and enjoys spending time in nature.

Values: Brady's values are reflected in his professional and personal endeavors. His commitment to discipline, hard work, and continual improvement is evident in his approach to football and his health and wellness practices. He also values teamwork and leadership, as seen through his role as a quarterback and his ability to inspire and motivate his teammates. Brady has spoken about the importance of resilience, a trait that has helped him overcome challenges and setbacks throughout his career. In his personal life, he emphasizes the importance of family, kindness, and giving back to the community.

In conclusion, Tom Brady's personal life reflects a blend of strong family bonds, diverse interests, and deeply held values. These elements have not only influenced his success on the football field but have also shaped his contributions off the field.

Printed in Great Britain
by Amazon

25074472R00059